A PHOENIX TOO FREQUENT was first produced at the Mercury Theatre, London, on April 25, 1946. It was directed by E. Martin Browne.

DYNAMENE ....Hermione Hannen
DOTO ....Eleanor Summerfield
TEGEUS-CHROMIS ....Alan Wheatley

SCENE

The tomb of Virilius, near Ephesus; night

NOTE

The story was got from Jeremy Taylor who had it from Petronius.

The setting of the play as described in the present text is that used by the author in his production at the Dolphin Theatre, Brighton. The setting was designed and built by Stewart Marshall.

3

A PHOENIX TOO FREQUENT

*The curtain rises on a stage in almost total darkness. The
set is an underground tomb, and the only light at first
comes from a very low dim flame in an oil lamp. As the
light from the lamp and the starry sky overhead increases,
the shape and furniture of the tomb are gradually per-
ceived. The stage is semicircular, and the up stage walls,
R. and L., are masked by plain curtains or drapes, hung
in folds. Down R. is the only entrance, an arched door-
way, leading down to stage level by a flight of stone
steps. Down C. is a stone or marble plinth, resembling the
lowest part of a classic column. On top of this stands a
simple stone urn. Down L. is a fairly large plinth or other
similar base on which lies a stone coffin. Up C. is a "flat"
extending from the stage floor up to the top of the set.
Cut into this, and large enough to show a person passing
by, is a sort of simple framework or grill. The stage set
has no roof or covering and above this, very dimly
lighted, is the suggestion of a sky at night, with a slight
shimmering from the starry sky. Above the top of the
curtains or drapes, between U. C. and L. C., there is a
cut-out or stencil-like suggestion or the branches of two
or three trees, and from these a further suggestion of six
soldiers who have been hanged from the branches. The
night sky should be extended over the rest of the set as
seen to the right. The entrance to the tomb is so arranged
as to permit a suggestion of starlight or moonlight. A
rock, large enough to be used as a stool, is down R. below
the lowest of the steps leading to the door.
A few seconds after the rise of the curtain DOTO is seen
standing by the lamp, which is placed on the top step
leading from the entrance right. DYNAMENE leans on the
R. of the coffin plinth.*

5

DOTO.

Nothing but the harmless day gone into black
Is all the dark is. And so what's my trouble?
Demons is so much wind. Are so much wind.
I've plenty to fill my thoughts. All that I ask
Is don't keep turning men over in my mind,
Venerable Aphrodite. I've had my last one
And thank you. I thank thee. He smelt of sour grass
And was likeable. He collected ebony quoits.
(*An owl hoots near at hand.*)
O Zeus! O some god or other, where is the oil?
(*Rises, goes* U. S.)
Fire's from Prometheus. (*Back to lamp.*) I thank thee. If I
Mean to die I'd better see what I'm doing.
(*She fills the lamp with oil. The flame burns up brightly and
shows* DYNAMENE, *beautiful and young, leaning asleep beside
a bier.*)
Honestly, I would rather have to sleep
With a bald bee-keeper who was wearing his boots
Than spend more days fasting and thirsting and crying
In a tomb. I shouldn't have said that. Pretend
I didn't hear myself. But life and death
Is cat and dog in this double-bed of a world.
My master, my poor master, was a man
Whose nose was as straight as a little buttress,
And now he has taken it into Elysium
Where it won't be noticed among all the other straightness.
(*The owl cries again and wakens* DYNAMENE.)
Oh, them owls. Those owls. It's woken her. (*Crosses* L.)

DYNAMENE.

Ah! I'm breathless. I caught up with the ship
But it spread its wings, creaking a cry of *Dew,*
Dew! and flew figurehead foremost into the sun.

DOTO.

How crazy, madam.

DYNAMENE.

              Doto, draw back the curtains.
I'll take my barley-water.

DOTO.

              We're not at home
Now, madam. It's the master's tomb.

6

DYNAMENE.

Of course!

Oh, I'm wretched. Already I have disfigured
My vigil. My cynical eyelids have soon dropped me
In a dream.

DOTO.

But then it's possible (*Kneels to* DYNAMENE.),
madam, you might
Find yourself in bed with him again
In a dream, madam. Was he on the ship?

DYNAMENE.

He was the ship.

DOTO.

Oh. That makes it different.

DYNAMENE.

He was the ship. He had such a deck, Doto,
Such a white, scrubbed deck. Such a stern prow,
Such a proud stern, so slim from port to starboard.
If ever you meet a man with such fine masts
Give your life to him, Doto. The figurehead
Bore his own features, so serene in the brow
And hung with a little seaweed. O Virilius,
My husband, you have left a wake in my soul.
You cut the glassy water with a diamond keel.
I must cry again.

DOTO.

What, when you mean to join him?
Don't you believe he will be glad to see you, madam?
Thankful to see you, I should imagine, among
Them shapes and shades; all shapes of shapes and all
Shades of shades, from what I've heard. I know
I shall feel odd at first with Cerberus,
Sop or no sop. Still, I know how you feel, madam.
You think he may find a temptation in Hades.
I shouldn't worry. It would help him to settle down.
(DYNAMENE *weeps.*)
It would only be *fun*, madam. He couldn't go far
With a shade.

DYNAMENE.

He was one of the coming men.
He was certain to have become the most well-organized provost

7

The town has known, once they had made him provost.
He was so punctual, you could regulate
The sun by him. He made the world succumb
To his daily revolution of habit. But who,
In the world he has gone to, will appreciate that?
O poor Virilius! To be a coming man
Already gone—it must be distraction.
Why did you leave me walking about our ambitions
Like a cat in the ruins of a house? Promising husband,
Why did you insult me by dying? Virilius,
Now I keep no flower, except in the vase
Of the tomb.

DOTO.

O poor madam! O poor master!
I presume so far as to cry somewhat for myself
As well. I know you won't mind, madam. It's two
Days not eating makes me think of my uncle's
Shop in the country, where he has a hardware business,
Basins, pots, ewers, and alabaster birds.
He makes you die of laughing. O madam,
Isn't it sad?
(*They both weep.*)

DYNAMENE.

How could I have allowed you
To come and die of my grief? Doto, it puts
A terrible responsibility on me. Have you
No grief of your own you could die of?

DOTO.

Not really, madam.

DYNAMENE.

Nothing?

DOTO.

Not really. They was all one to me.
Well, all but two was all one to me. And they,
Strange enough, was two who kept recurring.
I could never be sure if they had gone for good
Or not; and so that kept things cheerful, madam.
One always gave a wink before he deserted me,
The other slapped me as it were behind, madam;
Then they would be away for some months.

DYNAMENE.

Oh, Doto,

What an unhappy life you were having to lead.

DOTO.

Yes, I'm sure. But never mind, madam,
It seemed quite lively then. And now I know
It's what you say; life is more big than a bed
And full of miracles and mysteries like
One man made for one woman, etcetera, etcetera.
Lovely. I feel sung, madam, by a baritone
In mixed company with everyone pleased.
And so I had to come with you here, madam,
For the last sad chorus of me. It's all
Fresh to me. Death's a new interest in life,
If it doesn't disturb you, madam, to have me crying.
It's because of us not having breakfast again.
And the master, of course. And the beautiful world.
And you crying too, madam. Oh—Oh!

DYNAMENE.

I can't forbid your crying; but you must cry
On the other side of the tomb. I'm becoming confused.
(DOTO *rises, walks over* R.)
This is my personal grief and my sacrifice
Of self, solus. Right over there, darling girl.

DOTO.

What here?

DYNAMENE.

Now, if you wish, you may cry, Doto.

(*Rises and goes* U. S.)
But our tears are very different. For me
The world is all with Charon, all, all,
Even the metal and plume of the rose garden,
And the forest where the sea fumes overhead
In vegetable tides, and particularly
The entrance to the warm baths in Arcite Street
Where we first met;—all!—the sun itself
Trails an evening hand in the sultry river
Far away down by Acheron. I am lonely,
Virilius. (*Sits on* U. S. *end of coffin plinth.*) Where is the
   punctual eye
And where is the cautious voice which made

9

Balance-sheets sound like Homer and Homer sound
Like balance-sheets? The precision of limbs, the amiable
Laugh, the exact festivity? Gone from the world.
You were the peroration of nature, Virilius.
You explained everything to me, even the extremely
Complicated gods. You wrote them down
In seventy columns. Dear curling calligraphy!
Gone from the world, once and for all. And I taught you
(Rises.)
In your perceptive moments to appreciate me.
You said I was harmonious, Virilius,
Moulded and harmonious, little matronal
Ox-eye, your package. (Moves R. in circular move.) And
then I would walk
Up and down largely, as it were making my own
Sunlight. (Back to coffin.) What a mad blacksmith (Moves R.)
creation is
Who blows his furnaces until the stars fly upward
And iron Time is hot and politicians glow
And bulbs and roots sizzle into hyacinth
And orchis, and the sand puts out the lion,
Roaring yellow, and oceans bud with porpoises,
Blenny, tunny and the almost unexisting
Blindfish; throats are cut, the masterpiece
Looms out of labor; nations and rebellions
Are spat out to hang on the wind—(Back to D. S. end of
plinth.) and all is gone
In one Virilius, wearing his office tunic,
Checking the pence column as he went.
Where's animation now? What is there that stays
To dance? The eye of the one-eyed world is out. (Kneels at
coffin. She weeps.)

DOTO.

I shall try to grieve a little, too.
It would take lessons, I imagine, to do it out loud
For long. If I could only remember
Any one of those fellows without wanting to laugh.
Hopeless, I am. Now those good pair of shoes
I gave away without thinking, that's a different—
Well, I've cried enough about them, I suppose.
Poor madam, poor master.

(TEGEUS *comes through the gate to the top of the steps.*)

TEGEUS.

What's your trouble?

DOTO.

Oh!

Oh! Oh, a man. I thought for a moment it was something
With harm in it. Trust a man to be where it's dark.
What is it? Can't you sleep?

TEGEUS.

Now, listen—

DOTO.

Hush!

Remember you're in the grave. You must go away.
Madam is occupied.

TEGEUS.

What, here?

DOTO.

Becoming

Dead. We both are.

TEGEUS.

What's going on here?

DOTO.

Grief.

Are you satisfied now?

TEGEUS.

Less and less. Do you know

What the time is?

DOTO.

I'm not interested.

We've done with all that. Go away. Be a gentleman.
If we can't be free of men in a grave
Death's a dead loss.

TEGEUS.

It's two in the morning. All

I ask is what are women doing down here
At two in the morning?

DOTO.

Can't you see she's crying?

Or is she sleeping again? Either way
She's making arrangements to join her husband.

11

TEGEUS.

Where?

DOTO.

Good god, in the Underworld, dear man. Haven't you learnt
About life and death?

TEGEUS.

In a manner, yes; in a manner;
The rudiments. So the lady means to die?

DOTO.

For love; beautiful, curious madam.

TEGEUS.

Not curious;
I've had thoughts like it. Death is a kind of love.
Not anything I can explain.

DOTO.

You'd better come in
And sit down. (*Sits* C., R. *side.*)

TEGEUS.

I'd be grateful. (*Sits* R. *on stool.*)

DOTO.

Do. It will be my last
Chance to have company, in the flesh.

TEGEUS.

Do you mean
You're going too?

DOTO.

Oh, certainly I am.
Not anything I can explain.
It all started with madam saying a man
Was two men really, and I'd only noticed one,
One each, I mean. It seems he has a soul
As well as his other troubles. And I like to know
What I'm getting with a man. I'm inquisitive,
I suppose you'd call me.

TEGEUS.

It takes some courage.

DOTO.

Well, yes
And no. I'm fond of change.

TEGEUS.

Would you object
To have me eating my supper here? (*Takes food out.*)

DOTO.

Be careful
Of the crumbs. We don't want a lot of squeaking mice
Just when we're dying.

TEGEUS.

What a sigh she gave them. (*Rises.*)
Down the air like a slow comet.
And now she's all dark again. Mother of me.
How long has this been going on?

DOTO.

Two days.
It should have been three by now, but at first
Madam had difficulty with the Town Council. They said
They couldn't have a tomb used as a private residence.
But madam told them she wouldn't be eating here,
Only suffering, and they thought that would be all right.

TEGEUS.

Two of you. Marvellous. (*Sits.*) Who would have said
I should ever have stumbled on anything like this?
Do you have to cry? Yes, I suppose so. It's all
Quite reasonable.

DOTO.

Your supper and your knees.
That's what's making me cry. I can't hear sympathy
And they're sympathetic.

TEGEUS.

Please eat a bit of something.
I've no appetite left.

DOTO.

And see her go ahead of me?
Wrap it up; put it away. You sex of wicked beards!
It's no wonder you have to shave off your black souls
Every day as they push through your chins.
I'll turn my back on you. It means utter
Contempt. Eat? Utter contempt. Oh, little new rolls!
(*To* R. *end of* C. *plinth.*)

TEGEUS.

Forget it, forget it; please forget it. Remember

13

I've had no experience of this kind of thing before.
(*Rises, crosses* L. *to back of* DOTO.)
Indeed I'm as sorry as I know how to be. (*Puts food down.*)
Ssh,
We'll disturb her. She sighed again. O Zeus,
It's terrible! Asleep, and still sighing.
Mourning has made a warren in her spirit,
All that way below. Ponos! the heart
Is the devil of a medicine.

DOTO.

And I don't intend
To turn round.

TEGEUS.

I understand how you must feel.
Would it be—have you any objection
To my having a drink? I have a little wine here.
And, you probably see how it is: grief's in order,
(*To* R. *end of plinth.*)
And death's in order, and women—I can usually
Manage that too; but not all three together
At this hour of the morning. So you'll excuse me.
(U. S. *to get drink.*)
How about you? It would make me more comfortable
If you'd take a smell of it.

DOTO.

One for the road?

TEGEUS.

One for the road. (*Pours drinks.*)

DOTO.

It's the dust in my throat. The tomb
Is so dusty. Thanks, I will. (*Takes drink.*) There's no point
in dying
Of everything, simultaneous. (*Rises.*)

TEGEUS.

It's lucky
I brought two bowls. I was expecting to keep
A drain for my relief when he comes in the morning.

DOTO.

Are you on duty? (*To* TEGEUS R.)

TEGEUS.

Yes.

14

DOTO.

It looks like it.

TEGEUS.

Well,

Here's your good health.

DOTO.

What good is that going to do me?
Here's to an easy crossing and not too much waiting
About on the bank. Do you have to tremble like that?

TEGEUS.

The idea—I can't get used to it.

DOTO.

For a member
Of the forces, you're peculiarly queasy. (*An owl hoots.*) I
   wish
Those owls were in Hades—oh, no; let them stay where they
   are.
Have you never had nothing to do with corpses before?

TEGEUS.

I've got six of them outside.

DOTO.

Morpheus, that's plenty.
What are they doing here?

TEGEUS.

Hanging.

DOTO.

Hanging?

TEGEUS.

On trees.
Five plane trees and a holly. The holly-berries
Are just reddening. Another drink?

DOTO.

Why not?

TEGEUS.

It's from Samos. Here's—

DOTO.

All right. Let's just drink it.
—How did they get in that predicament?

TEGEUS.

The sandy-haired fellow said (*To bannister.*) we should collaborate

15

With everybody; the little man said he wouldn't
Collaborate with anybody; the old one
Said that the Pleiades weren't sisters but cousins
And anyway were manufactured in Lacedaemon.
The fourth said that we hanged men for nothing.
The other two said nothing. Now they hang
About at the corner of the night, they're present
And absent, horribly obsequious to every
Move in the air, and yet they keep me standing
For five hours at a stretch.

DOTO.

                       The wine has gone
Down to my knees. (*Sits* R. *end of plinth.*)

TEGEUS.

                And up to your cheeks. You're looking
Fresher. If only—

DOTO.

              Madam? She never would.
Shall I ask her? (*Half rises.*)

TEGEUS.

              No; no, don't dare, don't breathe it.
(*Crosses* L. *behind, sits on* L. *side of plinth.*)
This is privilege, to come so near
To what is undeceiving and uncorrupt
And undivided; this is the clear fashion
For all souls, a ribbon to bind the unruly
Curls of living, a faith, a hope, Zeus
Yes, a fine thing. I am human, and this
Is human fidelity, and we can be proud.
And unphilosophical.

DOTO.

              I need to dance
But I haven't the use of my legs.

TEGEUS.

                  No, no, don't dance,
Or, at least, only inwards; don't dance; cry
Again. We'll put a moat of tears
Round her bastion of love, and save
The world. It's something, it's more than something,
It's regeneration, to see how a human cheek
Can become as pale as a pool.

DOTO.

Do you love me, handsome?

TEGEUS.

To have found life, after all, unambiguous!

DOTO.

Did you say Yes?

TEGEUS.

Certainly; just now I love all men. (*Rises.*)

DOTO.

So do I.

TEGEUS.

And the world is a good creature again.
I'd begun to see it as mildew, verdigris,
Rust, woodrot, or as though the sky had uttered
An oval twirling blasphemy with occasional vistas
In country districts. I was within an ace
Of volunteering for overseas service. Despair
Abroad can always nurse pleasant thoughts of home.
Integrity, by god!

DOTO.

I love all the world (*Rises.*)
And the movement of the apple in your throat.
So shall you kiss me? It would be better, I should think,
To go moistly to Hades.

TEGEUS.

Hers is the way,
Luminous with sorrow.

DOTO.

Then I'll take

(*To helmet, by bannister* R.)
Another little swiggy. I love all men,
Everybody, even you, and I'll pick you
Some outrageous honeysuckle for your helmet,
If only it lived here. Pardon.

DYNAMENE.

Doto. Who is it?

(TEGEUS *crosses* R. *to about.*)

DOTO.

Honeysuckle, madam. (*Crosses* L. *in front.*) Because of the
bees.
Go back to sleep, madam.

17

DYNAMENE.

What person is it?

DOTO.

Yes, I see what you mean, madam. It's a kind of
Corporal talking to his soul, on a five-hour shift,
Madam, with six bodies. He's been having his supper.
(*Crossing* L. *to* DOTO *and taking her* U. S.)

TEGEUS.

I'm going. It's terrible that we should have disturbed her.

DOTO.

He was delighted to see you so sad, madam.
It has stopped him going abroad.

DYNAMENE.

One with six bodies?
A messenger, a guide to where we go.
(TEGEUS *brings* DOTO *down and crosses* R.)
It is possible he has come to show us the way
Out of these squalid suburbs of life, a shade,
A gorgon, who has come swimming up, against
The falls of my tears (for which in truth he would need
Many limbs) to guide me to Virilius.
I shall go quietly. (*Behind plinth and* R. *to* TEGEUS.)

TEGEUS.

I do assure you—
Such clumsiness, such a vile and unforgivable
Intrusion. I shall obliterate myself
Immediately.

DOTO.

Oblit—oh, what a pity
To oblit. Pardon. Don't let him, the nice fellow.
(*Sits* L. *end plinth.*)

DYNAMENE.

Sir: your other five bodies: where are they?

Madam—

TEGEUS.

Outside; I have them outside. On trees.

DYNAMENE.

Quack!

TEGEUS.

What do I reply?

18

DYNAMENE.

Quack, charlatan!

(TEGEUS *retreats back* R. *to stove.*)
You've never known the gods. You came to mock me.
Doto, this never was a gorgon, never.
Nor a gentleman either. He's completely spurious.
Admit it, you creature. Have you even a feather
Of the supernatural in your system? Have you?
(*Sits* R. *end of plinth.*)

TEGEUS.

Some of my relations—

DYNAMENE.

Well?

TEGEUS.

Are dead, I think;

That is to say I have connexions—(*Sits stone* R.)

DYNAMENE.

Connexions

With pickpockets. It's a shameless imposition.
Does the army provide you with no amusements?
If I were still of the world, and not cloistered
In a colorless landscape of winter thought
Where the approaching Spring is desired oblivion,
I should write sharply to your commanding officer.
It should be done, it should be done. If my fingers
Weren't so cold I would do it now. But they are,
Horribly cold. (*She rises and moves* U. S.) And why should
  insolence matter
When my color of life is unreal, a blush on death,
A partial mere diaphane? I don't know
Why it should matter. (*Down to plinth.*) Oafish, non-com-
  missioned
Young man! The boots of your conscience will pinch for ever
If life's dignity has any self-protection.
Oh, I have to sit down. (*Sits* R. *end of plinth.*) The tomb's
  going round.

DOTO.

Oh, madam, don't give over. I can't remember (*Rises.*)
When things were so lively. He looks marvellously
Marvellously uncomfortable. Go on, madam.
Can't you, madam? Oh, madam, don't you feel up to it?

(*Crosses* R. *in front of* TEGEUS.)

There, do you see her, you acorn-chewing infantryman?
You've made her cry, you square-bashing barbarian.

TEGEUS. (*Crosses* L. *behind and sits* L. *end plinth.*)

O history, my private history, why
Was I led here? What stigmatism has got
Into my stars? Why wasn't it my brother?
He has a tacit misunderstanding with everybody
.And washes in it. Why wasn't it my mother?
She makes a collection of other people's tears
And dries them all. (*Rises, crosses* R. *to foot of steps.*) Let
　　them forget I came;
And lie in the terrible black crystal of grief
Which held them, before I broke it. Outside, Tegeus.

DOTO.

Hey, I don't think so, I shouldn't say so. Come (*To* TEGEUS.)
Down again, uniform. Do you think you're going
To half kill an unprotected lady and then
Back out upwards? Do you think you can leave her like this?

TEGEUS.

Yes, yes, I'll leave her. O directorate of gods,
How can I? Beauty's bit is between my teeth.
She has added another torture to me. Bottom
Of Hades' bottom.

DOTO.

　　　　　　　　Madam, Madam, the corporal
Has some wine here. It will revive you, madam.
And then you can go at him again, madam.

TEGEUS. (*Moving down to* DYNAMENE.)

It's the opposite of everything you've said,
I swear. I swear by Horkos and the Styx,
I swear by the nine acres of Tityos,
I swear the Hypnotic oath, by all the Titans—
By Koeos, Krios, Iapetos, Kronos, and so on—
By the three Hekatoncheires, by the insomnia
Of Tisiphone, by Jove, by jove, and the dew
On the feet of my boyhood, I am innocent
Of mocking you. Am I a Salmoneus
That, seeing such a flame of sorrow—

20

DYNAMENE.

You needn't
Labor to prove your secondary education.
Perhaps I jumped to a wrong conclusion, perhaps
I was hasty.

DOTO.

How easy to swear if you're properly educated.
Wasn't it pretty, madam? Pardon.

DYNAMENE.

If I misjudged you
I apologize, I apologize. Will you please leave us?
You were wrong to come here. In a place of mourning
Light itself is a trespasser; nothing can have
The right of entrance except those natural symbols
Of mortality, the jabbing, funeral, sleek—
With-omen raven, the death-watch beetle which mocks
Time: particularly, I'm afraid, the spider
(*Watching spider on floor moving* L. *of coffin.*)
Weaving his home with swift self-generated
Threads of slaughter; and, of course, the worm.
I wish it could be otherwise. Oh dear,
They aren't easy to live with.

DOTO. (*Crossing* L. *to* DYNAMENE.)

Not even a *little* wine, madam?

DYNAMENE.

Here, Doto?

DOTO.

Well, on the steps perhaps,
Except it's so draughty.

DYNAMENE.

Doto! Here?

DOTO.

No, madam;
I quite see.

DYNAMENE.

I might be wise to strengthen myself
In order to fast again; it would make me abler
For grief. I will breathe a little of it, Doto.
(*Crosses, sits on* L. *end of plinth.*)

DOTO.

Thank god. Where's the bottle? (*Gets bottle from* R.)

21

DYNAMENE. (*Picking up bowl, which has been left on plinth.*)
     What an exquisite bowl.
TEGEUS.
     Now that it's peacetime we have pottery classes.
DYNAMENE.
     You made it yourself?
TEGEUS.
                              Yes. Do (*To* DYNAMENE.) you see the
     design?
     The corded god, tied also by the rays
     Of the sun, and the astonished ship erupting
     Into vines and vine-leaves, inverted pyramids
     Of grapes, the uplifted hands of the men (the raiders),
     And here the headlong sea, itself almost
     Venturing into leaves and tendrils, and Proteus
     With his beard braiding the wind, and this
     Held by other hands is a drowned sailor—
DYNAMENE.
     Always, always.
DOTO. (*Pouring drink.*)
                              Hold the bowl steady, madam.
     Pardon.
DYNAMENE.
     Doto, have you been drinking? (*Rising.*)
DOTO.
                                        Here, madam?
     I coaxed some a little way towards my mouth, madam,
     But I scarcely swallowed except because I had to. The hiccup
     Is from no breakfast, madam, and not meant to be funny.
     (*Gives bowl to* DOTO *and breaks* L. *to coffin.*)
DYNAMENE.
     You may drink this too. Oh, how the inveterate body,
     Even when cut from the heart, insists on leaf,
     Puts out, with a separate meaningless will,
     Fronds to intercept the thankless sun.
     How it does, oh, how it does. And how it confuses
     The nature of the mind.
TEGEUS.
                              Yes, yes, the confusion;
     (*Sits* L. *end of plinth.*)
     That's something I understand better than anything.

22

DYNAMENE. (*Turning to* TEGEUS.)
  When the thoughts would die, the instincts will set sail
  For life. And when the thoughts are alert for life
  The instincts will rage to be destroyed on the rocks.
  (*Turning toward coffin.*)
  To Virilius it was not so; his brain was an ironing-board
  For all crumpled indecision: and I follow him,
  The hawser of my world. You don't belong here,
  You see; you don't belong here at all.
TEGEUS. (*Rising, crossing* L. *to* DYNAMENE.)
                                       If only
  I did. If only you knew the effort it costs me
  To mount those steps again into an untrustworthy,
  Unpredictable, unenlightened night,
  And turn my back on—on a state of affairs,
  I can only call it a vision, a hope, a promise,
  A —— (*Backing toward steps.*) By that I mean loyalty, en·
    during passion,
  Unrecking bravery and beauty all in one.
DOTO.
  He means you, or you and me; or me, madam.
TEGEUS.
  It only remains for me to thank you, and to say
  That whatever awaits me and for however long
  I may be played by this poor musician, existence,
  Your person and sacrifice will leave their trace
  As clear upon me as the shape of the hills
  (*Quick move to bottom of steps.*)
  Around my birthplace. Now I must leave you to your husband.
DOTO.
  Oh! You, madam.
DYNAMENE.
                        I'll tell you what I will do.
  (*Crossing* R. *to* TEGEUS.)
  I will drink with you to the memory of my husband,
  Because I have been curt, because you are kind,
  And because I'm extremely thirsty. And then we will say
  Good-bye and part to go to our opposite corruptions,
  The world and the grave.
  (*She takes bowl and moves* L. *to* C. DOTO *moves* R., *takes
    bottle.*)

23

TEGEUS.

The climax to the vision.

(*He takes bowl, goes to* DYNAMENE.)

DYNAMENE. (*Drinking.*)

My husband, and all he stood for.

TEGEUS.

Stands for.

DYNAMENE.

Stands for.

TEGEUS.

Your husband.

DOTO.

The master. (*Sits on rock,* R.)

DYNAMENE.

How good it is,
How it sings to the throat, purling with summer.

TEGEUS.

It has a twin nature, winter and warmth in one,
Moon and meadow. Do you agree?

DYNAMENE.

Perfectly;
A cold bell sounding in a golden month.

TEGEUS.

Crystal in harvest.

DYNAMENE.

Perhaps a nightingale
Sobbing among the pears.

TEGEUS.

In an old autumnal midnight.

DOTO.

Grapes.—Pardon. There's some more here.

TEGEUS.

Plenty.
I drink to the memory of your husband.

DYNAMENE.

My husband.

DOTO.

The master.

DYNAMENE.

He was careless in his choice of wines. (*Sits* L. *end.*)

24

TEGEUS.

                                                            And yet

    Rendering to living its rightful poise is not
    Unimportant. (*Placing his foot on* R. *end of plinth*.)

DYNAMENE.

                        A mystery's in the world
    Where a little liquid, with flavor, quality, and fume
    Can be as no other, can hint and flute our senses
    As though a music played in harvest hollows
    And a movement was in the swathes of our memory.
    (*Putting her arm on* TEGEUS' *knee*.)
    Why should scent, why should flavor come
    With such wings upon us? Parsley, for instance.
    (*Realizing what she is doing, and taking away her arm*.)

TEGEUS.

    Seaweed.

DYNAMENE.

            Lime trees.

DOTO.

                        Horses.

TEGEUS.

                            Fruit in the fire.

DYNAMENE.

    Do I know your name?

TEGEUS.

                        Tegeus. (*Sitting* R. *end*.)

DYNAMENE.

                                That's very thin for you,
    It hardly covers your bones. Something quite different,
    Altogether other. I shall think of it presently.

TEGEUS.

                            Darker vowels, perhaps.

DYNAMENE.

                            Yes, certainly darker vowels.
    And your consonants should have a slight angle,
    And a certain temperature. Do you know what I mean?
    It will come to me.

TEGEUS.

                    Now *your* name—

DYNAMENE.

It is nothing
To any purpose. I'll be to you the She
In the tomb. You have the air of a natural-historian
As though you were accustomed to handling birds' eggs,
Or tadpoles, or putting labels on moths. You see?
The genius of dumb things, that they are nameless.
Have I found the seat of the weevil in human brains?
Our names. They make us broody; we sit and sit
To hatch them into reputation and dignity.
And then they set upon us and become despair,
Guilt and remorse. We go where they lead. We dance
Attendance on something wished upon us by the wife
Of our mother's physician. But insects meet and part
And put the woods about them, fill the dusk
And freckle the light and go and come without
A name among them, without the wish of a name
And very pleasant too. Did I interrupt you?

TEGEUS.

I forget. We'll have no names then.

DYNAMENE.

I should like
You to have a name, I don't know why; a small one
To fill out the conversation.

TEGEUS.

I should like
You to have a name too, if only for something
To remember. Have you still some wine in your bowl?

DYNAMENE.

Not altogether.

TEGEUS.

We haven't come to the end
By several inches. Did I splash you?

DYNAMENE.

It doesn't matter.
Well, here's to my husband's name.

TEGEUS.

Your husband's name.

DOTO.

The master.

26

DYNAMENE.
It was kind of you to come.

TEGEUS.
It was more than coming. I followed my future here,
As we all do if we're sufficiently inattentive
And don't vex ourselves with questions; or do I mean
Attentive? If so, attentive to what? Do I sound
Incoherent?

DYNAMENE.
You're wrong. There isn't a future here,
Not here, not for you.

TEGEUS.
Your name's Dynamene.

DYNAMENE.
Who—Have I been utterly· irreverent? Are you—
Who made you say that? Forgive me the question,
But are you dark or light? I mean which shade
(*Rising, going behind plinth to* DYNAMENE.)
Of the supernatural? Or if neither, what prompted you?

TEGEUS.
Dynamene ——

DYNAMENE.
No, but I'm sure you're the friend of nature,
It must be so, I think I see little Phoebuses
Rising and setting in your eyes.

DOTO.
They're not little Phoebuses,
They're hoodwinks, madam. Your name is on your brooch.
No little Phoebuses tonight.

DYNAMENE.
That's twice.
(*Moving away* U. S. L.)
You've played me a trick. Oh, I know practical jokes
Are common on Olympus, but haven't we at all
Developed since the gods were born? Are gods
And men both to remain immortal adolescents?
How tiresome it all is.

TEGEUS. (*Moving* U. S. *to* DYNAMENE.)
It was you, each time,
Who said I was supernatural. When did I say so?

27

(DYNAMENE *moves down,* TEGEUS *follows.*)
You're making me into whatever you imagine
And then you blame me because I can't live up to it.
DYNAMENE.

I shall call you Chromis. It has a breadlike sound.
I think of you as a crisp loaf.
TEGEUS.

And now
You'll insult me because I'm not sliceable.
(*Crossing* R., *sitting* L. *end of plinth.*)
DYNAMENE.

I think drinking is harmful to our tempers.
TEGEUS.

If I seem to be frowning, that is only because
I'm looking directly into your light: I must look
Angrily, or shut my eyes.
DYNAMENE.

Shut them.—(*Moving* R.) Oh,
You have eyelashes! A new perspective of you.
Is that how you look when you sleep?
(*Flood creeps on from outside.*)
TEGEUS.

My jaw drops down.
DYNAMENE.

Show me how.
TEGEUS.

Like this.
DYNAMENE.

It makes an irresistible
Moron of you. Will you waken now? (*Crossing* R. *behind.*)
It's morning; I see a thin dust of daylight
Blowing on to the steps.
TEGEUS.

Already? (*Rising.*) Dynamene,
You're tricked again. This time by the moon.
DYNAMENE.

Oh, well,
Moon's daylight, then. Doto is asleep.
TEGEUS.

Doto
Is asleep .

28

DYNAMENE.

Chromis, what made you walk about
(Moving down, sitting R. end of plinth.)
In the night? What, I wonder, made you not stay
Sleeping wherever you slept? Was it the friction
Of the world on your mind? Those two are difficult
To make agree. Chromis—now try to learn
To answer your name. I won't say Tegeus.

TEGEUS.

And I

Won't say Dynamene.

DYNAMENE.

Not?

TEGEUS.

It makes you real.
Forgive me, a terrible thing has happened. *(Breaks L.)* Shall I
Say it and perhaps destroy myself for you?
Forgive me first, or, more than that, forgive
Nature who winds her furtive stream all through
Our reason. Do you forgive me?

DYNAMENE.

I'll forgive
Anything, if it's the only way I can know
What you have to tell me.

TEGEUS. *(Turning to* DYNAMENE, *head down.)*

I felt us to be alone;
Here in a grave, separate from any life,
I and the only one of beauty, the only
Persuasive key to all my senses, *(Head up.)*
In spite of my having lain day after day
And pored upon the sepals, corolla, stamen, and bracts
Of the yellow bog-iris. Then my body ventured
A step towards interrupting your perfection of purpose
And my own renewed faith in human nature.
Would you have believed that possible?

DYNAMENE.

I have never
Been greatly moved by the yellow bog-iris. Alas,
It's as I said. This place is for none but the spider,
Raven and worms, not for a living man.

TEGEUS.

    It has been a place of blessing to me. It will always
Play in me, a fountain of confidence
When the world is arid. But I know it is true
I have to leave it, and though it withers my soul
I must let you make your journey.
    (*Moving* R., *behind, to go.*)

DYNAMENE.

                     No.

TEGEUS.

                  Not true?

DYNAMENE.

    We can talk of something quite different.

TEGEUS.

                     Yes, we can!
Oh, yes, we will! Is it your opinion (*Moving* L. *behind.*)
That no one believes who hasn't learned to doubt?
Or, another thing, if we persuade ourselves
To one particular Persuasion, become Sophist,
Stoic, Platonist, anything whatever,
Would you say that there must be areas of soul
Lying unproductive therefore, or dishonored
Or blind?

DYNAMENE.

       No, I don't know.

TEGEUS.

                No. It's impossible
To tell. Dynamene, if only I had (*Sitting* L. *end of plinth.*)
Two cakes of pearl-barley and hydromel
I could see you to Hades, leave you with your husband
And come back to the world.

DYNAMENE.

              Ambition, I suppose,
Is an appetite particular to man. (*Turning away from* TEGEUS.)
What is your definition?

TEGEUS.

           The desire to find
A reason for living.

DYNAMENE.

          But then, suppose it leads,
As often, one way or another, it does, to death.

TEGEUS.

    Then that may be life's reason. Oh, but how
Could I bear to return, Dynamene? The earth's
Daylight would be my grave if I had left you
In that unearthly night.

DYNAMENE.

                    O Chromis —— (*Turning to* TEGEUS.)

TEGEUS.

                            Tell me,
(*Turning away to avoid kissing her.*)
What is your opinion of Progress? Does it, for example,
Exist? Is there ever progression without retrogression?
Therefore is it not true that mankind
Can more justly be said increasingly to Gress?
As the material improves, the craftsmanship deteriorates
And honor and virtue remain the same. I love you,
Dynamene.

DYNAMENE.

    Would you consider we go round and round?

TEGEUS.

    We concertina, I think; taking each time
A larger breath, so that the farther we go out
The farther we have to go in.

DYNAMENE.

                    There'll come a time
When it will be unbearable to continue.

TEGEUS.

    Unbearable.

DYNAMENE.

              Perhaps we had better have something
To eat. (TEGEUS *rises, crosses* R. *behind to get roll.*) The wine
   has made your eyes so quick
I am breathless beside them. It *is*
Your eyes, I think; or your intelligence
Holding my intelligence up above you
Between its hands. Or the cut of your uniform.

TEGEUS.

    Here's (*Crosses* L. *behind.*) a new roll with honey. In the
   gods' names
Let's sober ourselves. (*Handing roll to* DYNAMENE.)

DYNAMENE.

As soon as possible.

TEGEUS.

Have you
Any notion of algebra? (*Sitting on floor* L., *front of plinth.*)

DYNAMENE.

We'll discuss you, Chromis.
We will discuss you, till you're nothing but words.

TEGEUS.

I? There is nothing, of course, I would rather discuss,
Except—if it would be no intrusion—you, Dynamene.

DYNAMENE.

No, you couldn't want to. But your birthplace, Chromis,
With the hills that placed themselves in you for ever
As you say, where was it?

TEGEUS.

My father's farm at Pyxa.

DYNAMENE.

There? Could it be there?

TEGEUS.

I was born in the hills
Between showers, a quarter of an hour before milking time.
Do you know Pyxa? It stretches to the crossing of two
Troublesome roads, and buries its back in beechwood,
From which come the white owls of our nights
And the mulling and cradling of doves in the day.
I attribute my character to those shadows
And heavy roots; and my interest in music
To the sudden melodious escape of the young river
Where it breaks from nosing through the cresses and kingcups.
That's honestly so.

DYNAMENE.

You used to climb about
Among the windfallen tower of Phrasidemus
Looking for bees' nests.

TEGEUS.

What? When have I
Said so?

DYNAMENE.

Why, all the children did.

32

TEGEUS.

Yes: but, in the name of light, how do you know that?

DYNAMENE.

I played there once, on holiday.

TEGEUS. (Rising.)

O Klotho,

Lachesis and Atropos!

DYNAMENE.

It's the strangest chance:
I may have seen, for a moment, your boyhood.

TEGEUS.

I may
Have seen something like an early flower
Something like a girl. (Kneeling on floor to DYNAMENE.) If I
    only could remember how I must
Have seen you. Were you after the short white violets?
Maybe I blundered past you, taking your look,
And scarcely acknowledged how a star
Ran through me, to live in the brooks of my blood for ever.
Or I saw you playing at hiding in the cave
Where the ferns are and the water drips. (Rising.)

DYNAMENE.

I was quite plain and fat and I was usually
Hitting someone. I wish I could remember you.
I'm envious of the days and children who saw you
Then. It is curiously a little painful
Not to share your past.

TEGEUS.

How did it come
Our stars could mingle for an afternoon
So long ago, and then forget us or tease us
Or helplessly look on the dark high seas
Of our separation, while time drank
The golden hours? What hesitant fate is that?

DYNAMENE. (Rising, going u. s.)

Time? Time? Why—how old are we?

TEGEUS.

Young,
Thank both our mothers, but still we're older than tonight
And so older than we should be. Wasn't I born
In love with what, only now, I have grown to meet?

33

I'll tell you something else. I was born entirely
For this reason. I was born to fill a gap
In the world's experience, which had never known
Chromis loving Dynamene.

DYNAMENE. (*Down-stage on* R.)

You are so
Excited, poor Chromis. What is it? Here you are
With a woman who has wept away all claims
To appearance, unbecoming in her oldest clothes,
With not a trace of liveliness, a drab
Of melancholy, entirely shadow without
A smear of sun. Forgive me if I tell you
That you fall easily into superlatives.

TEGEUS.

Very well. I'll say nothing, then. I'll fume
With feeling. (*Turning away.*)

DYNAMENE.

Now you go to the extreme. Certainly
You must speak. You may have more to say. Besides
You might let your silence run away with you
And not say something that you should. And how
Should I answer you then? Chromis, you boy,
I can't look away from you. You use
The lamplight and the moon so skilfully,
So arrestingly, in and around your furrows.
A humorous ploughman goes whistling to a team
Of sad sorrow, to and fro in your brow
And over your arable cheek. Laugh for me. Have you
Cried for women, ever?

TEGEUS.

In looking about for you.
But I have recognized them for what they were.

DYNAMENE.

What were they?

TEGEUS. (*Standing on* L. *end of plinth.*)

Never you: never, although
They could walk with bright distinction into all men's
Longest memories, never you, by a hint
Or a faint quality, or at least not more
Than reflectively, stars lost and uncertain
In the sea, compared with the shining salt, the shiners,

34

The galaxies, the clusters, the bright grain whirling
Over the black threshing-floor of space.
Will you make some effort to believe that?

DYNAMENE.

No, no effort.
It lifts me and carries me. It may be wild
But it comes to me with a charm, like trust indeed,
And eats out of my heart, dear Chromis,
Absurd, disconcerting Chromis. You make me
Feel I wish I could look my best for you.
I wish, at least, that I could believe myself
To be showing some beauty for you, to put in the scales
(*Looking out front.*)
Between us. But they dip to you, they sink
With masculine victory.

TEGEUS.

Eros, no! No! (*Getting down.*)
If this is less than your best, then never, in my presence,
Be more than your less: never! If you should bring
More to your mouth or to your eyes, a moisture
Or a flake of light, anything, anything fatally
More, perfection would fetch her unsparing rod
Out of pickle to flay me, and what would have been love
Will be the end of me. O Dynamene,
Let me unload something of my lips' longing
On to yours receiving. Oh, when I cross
Like this the hurt of the little space between us
I come a journey from the wrenching ice
To walk in the sun. That is the feeling.

DYNAMENE.

Chromis,
Where am I going? No, don't answer. It's death
I desire, not you. (*Crossing* L.)

TEGEUS.

Where is the difference? Call me
Death instead of Chromis. I'll answer to anything.
It's desire all the same, of death in me, or me
In death, but Chromis either way. Is it so?
Do you not love me, Dynamene?

35

DYNAMENE.

How could it happen?
I'm going to my husband. I'm too far on the way
To admit myself to life again. Love's in Hades.

TEGEUS.

Also here. (*Crosses* L. *on* DYNAMENE'S L.) And here are we,
not there
In Hades. Is your husband expecting you?

DYNAMENE.

Surely, surely. (*Turning away, looking at coffin.*)

TEGEUS.

Not necessarily. I,
If I had been your husband, (DYNAMENE *turns away from*
coffin.) would never dream
Of expecting you. I should remember your body
Descending stairs in the floating light, but not
(TEGEUS *crosses to her* R.)
Descending in Hades. I should say "I have left
My wealth warm on the earth, and, hell, earth needs it."
"Was all I taught her of love," I should say, "so poor
That she will leave her flesh and become shadow?"
"Wasn't our love for each other" (I should continue)
"Infused with life, and life infused with our love?
Very well; repeat me in love, repeat me in life,
And let me sing in your blood for ever."

DYNAMENE.

Stop, stop, I shall be dragged apart!
(*To* C. *stage in front of plinth.*)
Why should the fates do everything to keep me
From dying honorably? They must have got
Tired of honor in Elysium. Chromis, it's terrible
To be susceptible to two conflicting norths.
I have the constitution of a whirlpool.
Am I actually twirling, or is it just sensation?

TEGEUS.

You're still; still as the darkness.

DYNAMENE.

What appears
Is so unlike what is. And what is madness
To those who only observe, is often wisdom
To those to whom it happens.

36

TEGEUS.

                              Are we compelled
To go into all this? (*Following* DYNAMENE.)

DYNAMENE.

                         Why, how could I return
To my friends? Am I to be an entertainment?

TEGEUS.

That's for tomorrow. Tonight I need to kiss you,
Dynamene. Let's see what the whirlpool does
Between my arms; let it whirl on my breast. O love,
Come in.

DYNAMENE.

I am there before I reach you; my body
Only follows to join my longing which
Is holding you already.—Now I am
All one again. (*They kiss.*)

TEGEUS.

                    I feel as the gods feel:
This is their sensation of life, not a man's:
Their suspension of immortality, to enrich
Themselves with time. O life, O death, O body,
O spirit, O Dynamene.

DYNAMENE.

                         O all
In myself; it so covets all in you,
My care, my Chromis. Then I shall be
Creation.

TEGEUS.

            You have the skies already;
Out of them you are buffeting me with your gales
Of beauty. Can we be made of dust, as they tell us?
What! dust with dust releasing such a light
And such an apparition of the world
Within one body? A thread of your hair has stung me.
Why do you push me away?

DYNAMENE.

                         There's so much metal
About you. Do I have to be imprisoned
In an armoury?

TEGEUS.

Give your hand to the buckles and then
To me.

DYNAMENE.

Don't help; I'll do them all myself. (*She undoes his armor.*)

TEGEUS.

O time and patience! I want you back again.

DYNAMENE.

We have a lifetime. O Chromis, think, think
Of that. And even unfastening a buckle
Is loving. And not easy. Very well,
You can help me. (TEGEUS *sits* L. *side of plinth.* DYNAMENE
kneels by him.) Chromis, what zone of miracle
Did you step into to direct you in the dark
To where I waited, not knowing I waited?

TEGEUS.

I saw
The lamplight. That was only the appearance
Of some great gesture in the bed of fortune.
I saw the lamplight.

DYNAMENE.

But here? So far from life?
What brought you near enough to see lamplight?

TEGEUS.

Zeus,
That reminds me.

DYNAMENE.

What is it, Chromis?

TEGEUS.

I'm on duty. (*Rises.*)

DYNAMENE.

Is it warm enough to do without your greaves?

TEGEUS.

Darling loom of magic, I must go back
To take a look at those boys. The whole business
Of guard had gone out of my mind.

DYNAMENE.

What boys, my heart?

TEGEUS.

My six bodies.

38

DYNAMENE.

Chromis, not that joke

Again.

TEGEUS.

No joke, sweet. Today our city
Held a sextuple hanging. I'm minding the bodies
Until five o'clock. Already I've been away
For half an hour.

DYNAMENE.

What can they do, poor bodies,

In half an hour, or half a century?
You don't really mean to go?

TEGEUS.

Only to make

My conscience easy. Then, Dynamene,
No cloud can rise on love, no hovering thought
Fidget, and the night will be only to *us*.

DYNAMENE.

But if every half-hour ——

TEGEUS.

Hush, (*Sits.*) smile of my soul,

My sprig, my sovereign: this is to hold your eyes,
I sign my lips on them both: this is to keep
Your forehead—do you feel the claim of my kiss
Falling into your thought? And now your throat
Is a white branch and my lips two singing birds—
They are coming to rest. Throat, remember me
Until I come back in five minutes. Over all
Here is my parole: I give it to your mouth
To give me again before it's dry. I promise:
Before it's dry, or not long after. (*Rising.*)

DYNAMENE.

Run, (*Rising.*)

Run all the way. You needn't be afraid of stumbling.
There's plenty of moon. The fields are blue. Oh, wait,
(TEGEUS *crosses* R. *to her.*)
Wait! My darling. No, not now: it will keep
Until I see you; I'll have it here at my lips. (*Crosses to him.*)
Hurry.

TEGEUS.

So long, my haven.

39

DYNAMENE.

Hurry, hurry! (*Exit* TEGEUS.)

DOTO.

Yes, madam, hurry; of course. Are we there
Already? How nice. Death doesn't take
Any doing at all. We were gulped into Hades
As easy as an oyster.

DYNAMENE.

Doto!

DOTO.

Hurry, hurry,
Yes, madam.—But they've taken out all my bones.
(*Trying to stand.*)
I haven't a bone left. I'm a Shadow: wonderfully shady
In the legs. We shall have to sit out eternity, madam,
If they've done the same to you.

DYNAMENE.

You'd better wake up.
If you can't go to sleep again, you'd better wake up.
Oh dear.—We're still alive, Doto, do you hear me?

DOTO.

You must speak for yourself, madam. I'm quite dead.
I'll tell you how I know. I feel
Invisible. (*Crossing* L. *with a birdlike movement to coffin.*)
I'm a wraith, madam; I'm only
Waiting to be wafted.

DYNAMENE. (*Moving* L. *to behind plinth.*)

If only you *would* be.
Do you see where you are? Look. Do you see?

DOTO.

Yes. You're right, madam. We're still alive.
Isn't it enough to make you swear?
Here we are, dying to be dead,
And where does it get us?

DYNAMENE.

Perhaps you should try to die
In some other place. Yes! Perhaps the air here
Suits you too well. You were sleeping very heavily.

DOTO.

And all the time you alone and dying.

40

I shouldn't have. Has the corporal been long gone,
Madam?

DYNAMENE.

He came and went, came and went,
You know the way. (*Breaking* R.)

DOTO.

Very well I do. And went
He should have, come he should never. Oh dear, he must
Have disturbed you, madam.

DYNAMENE.

He could be said
To've disturbed me. Listen; I have something to say to you.

DOTO.

I expect so, madam. Maybe I *could* have kept him out
But men are in before I wish they wasn't.
I think quickly enough, but I get behindhand
With what I ought to be saying. It's a kind of stammer
In my way of life, madam.

DYNAMENE.

I have been unkind,
I have sinfully wronged you, Doto. (*Crossing* L. *to* DOTO.)

DOTO.

Never, madam.

DYNAMENE.

Oh, yes. I was letting you die with me, Doto, without
Any fair reason. I was drowning you
In grief that wasn't yours. That was wrong, Doto.

DOTO.

But I haven't got anything against dying, madam.
I may *like* the situation, as far as I like
Any situation, madam. Now if you'd said mangling,
A lot of mangling, I might have thought twice about staying.
We all have our dislikes, madam.

DYNAMENE.

I'm asking you
To leave me, Doto, at once, as quickly as possible,
Now, before—now, Doto, and let me forget
My bad mind which confidently expected you
To companion me to Hades. Now good-bye,
Good-bye. (*Pushing* DOTO *toward entrance.*)

41

DOTO.

No, it's not good-bye at all. (*Moving* L. *again.*)
I shouldn't know another night of sleep, wondering
How you got on, or what I was missing, come to that.
I should be anxious about you, too. When you belong
To an upper class, the netherworld might come strange.
Now I was born nether, madam, though not
As nether as some. No, it's not good-bye, madam.
(*Sitting* L. *end of plinth.*)

DYNAMENE.

Oh, Doto, go; you must, you must! And if I seem
Without gratitude, forgive me. It isn't so,
(*Crossing* L. *to* DOTO.)
It is far, far from so. But I can only
Regain my peace of mind if I know you're gone.
(*Looking anxiously toward entrance.*)

DOTO.

Besides, look at the time, madam. Where should I go
At three in the morning? Even if I was to think
Of going; and think of it I never shall.

DYNAMENE.

Think of the unmatchable world, Doto.

DOTO.

I do
Think of it, madam. And when I think of it, what
Have I thought? Well, it depends, madam.

DYNAMENE.

I insist,
Obey me! At once! Doto!

DOTO.

Here I sit.

DYNAMENE.

What shall I do with you?
(*Moving behind plinth to entrance.*)

DOTO.

Ignore me, madam.
I know my place. I shall die quite unobtrusive.
(*Relaxing on plinth.*)
Oh, look, the corporal's forgotten to take his equipment.

DYNAMENE.

Could he be so careless?

42

DOTO.

I shouldn't hardly have thought so.
Poor fellow. They'll go and deduct it off his credits.
I suppose, madam, I suppose he couldn't be thinking
Of coming back?

DYNAMENE.

He'll think of these. He will notice
He isn't wearing them. He'll come; he is sure to come.
(*Looking out of entrance.*)

DOTO.
Oh.

DYNAMENE.
I know he will.

DOTO.

Oh, oh.
Is that all for tonight, madam? May I go now, madam?
(*Rising.*)

DYNAMENE.
Doto! Will you?

DOTO.

Just you try to stop me, madam.
Sometimes going is a kind of instinct with me.
I'll leave death to some other occasion.
(*Crossing* L. *to entrance.*)

DYNAMENE.

Do,
Doto. Any other time. Now you must hurry.
I won't delay you from life another moment.
Oh, Doto, good-bye.

DOTO.

Good-bye. Life is unusual,
Isn't it, madam? Remember me to Cerberus.
(*Re-enter* TEGEUS. DOTO *passes him on the steps.*
(*As she goes.*) You left something behind. Ye gods, what a
moon!

DYNAMENE.
Chromis, it's true; my lips are hardly dry.
Time runs again; the void is space again;
Space has life again; Dynamene has Chromis.

TEGEUS.
It's over. (*Sitting on rock* R. *of entrance.*)

43

DYNAMENE.

Chromis, you're sick. As white as wool.
(*By his side.*)
Come, you covered the distance too quickly.
Rest in my arms; get your breath again.

TEGEUS.

I've breathed one night too many. Why did I see you,
Why in the name of life did I see you?

DYNAMENE.

Why?
Weren't we gifted with each other? O heart,
What do you mean?

TEGEUS.

I mean that joy is nothing
But the parent of doom. Why should I have found
Your constancy such balm to the world and yet
Find, by the same vision, its destruction
A necessity? We're set upon by love
To make us incompetent to steer ourselves,
To make us docile to fate. I should have known:
Indulgences, not fulfilment, is what the world
Permits us.

DYNAMENE.

Chromis, is this intelligible?
Help me to follow you. What did you meet in the fields
To bring about all this talk? Do you still love me?

TEGEUS.

What good will it do us? I've lost a body.

DYNAMENE.

A body?
One of the six? Well, it isn't with them you propose
To love me; and you couldn't keep it for ever.
Are we going to allow a body that isn't there
To come between us?

TEGEUS.

But I'm responsible for it.
I have to account for it in the morning. (*Crossing* L. *to* L. *side
of plinth.*) Surely
You see, Dynamene, the horror we're faced with?
The relatives have had time to cut him down
And take him away for burial. It means

44

A court martial. No doubt about the sentence.
I shall take the place of the missing man.
To be hanged, Dynamene! Hanged, Dynamene!
(*Head on hands.*)

DYNAMENE.

No; it's monstrous! Your life is yours, Chromis.
(*Crossing to him.*)

TEGEUS.

Anything but. That's why I have to take it.
At the best we live our lives on loan,
At the worst in chains. And I was never born
To have life. Then for what? To be had by it,
And so are we all. But I'll make it what it is,
By making it nothing.

DYNAMENE.

Chromis, you're frightening me.
What are you meaning to do?

TEGEUS.

I have to die,
Dance of my heart, I have to die, to die,
To part us, to go to my sword and let it part us.
I'll have my free will even if I'm compelled to it.
I'll kill myself. (*Reaching for his sword.*)

DYNAMENE.

Oh, no! No, Chromis!
(*Taking sword, and backing L. to coffin, TEGEUS follows.*)
It's all unreasonable—no such horror
Can come of a pure accident. Have you hanged?
How can they hang you for simply not being somewhere?
How can they hang you for losing a dead man?
They must have wanted to lose him, or they wouldn't
Have hanged him. No, you're scaring yourself for nothing
And making me frantic.

TEGEUS.

It's section six, paragraph
Three in the Regulations. That's my doom.
I've read it for myself. And, by my doom,
Since I have to die, let me die here, in love,
Promoted by your kiss to tower, in dying,
High above my birth. For god's sake let me die
On a wave of life, Dynamene, with an action

45

I can take some pride in. How could I settle to death
Knowing that you last saw me stripped and strangled
On a holly tree? Demoted first and then hanged!
(*Moving* R. *to her.*)

DYNAMENE.

Am I supposed to love the corporal. (*Moving further down* L.)
Or you? It's you I love, from head to foot
And out to the ends of your spirit. What shall I do
If you die? How could I follow you? I should find you
Discussing me with my husband, comparing your feelings,
Exchanging reactions. Where should I put myself?
Or am I to live on alone, or find in life
Another source of love, in memory
Of Virilius and of you?

TEGEUS.

Dynamene, (*Crossing* L. *to her.*)
Not that! Since everything in the lives of men
Is brief to indifference, let our love at least
Echo and perpetuate itself uniquely
As long as time allows you. Though you go
To the limit of age, it won't be far to contain me.

DYNAMENE.

It will seem like eternity ground into days and days.

TEGEUS.

Can I be certain of you, for ever?

DYNAMENE.

But, Chromis,

Surely you said ——

TEGEUS.

Surely we have sensed
Our passion to be greater than mortal? Must I
Die believing it is dying with me?

DYNAMENE.

Chromis,

You must never die, never! It would be
An offence against truth.

TEGEUS.

I cannot live to be hanged.
It would be an offence against life. Give me my sword,
Dynamene. O Hades, when you look pale
You take the heart out of me. I could die

46

Without a sword by seeing you suffer. Quickly!
Give me my heart back again with your lips
And I'll live the rest of my ambitions
In a last kiss.

DYNAMENE.

Oh, no, no, no! (*Crossing* R. *to in front of plinth.*)
Give my blessing to your desertion of me?
Never, Chromis, never. Kiss you and then
Let you go? Love you, for death to have you?
Am I to be made the fool of courts martial?
Who are they who think they can discipline souls
Right off the earth? What discipline is that?
Chromis, love is the only discipline
And we're the disciples of love. I hold you to that:
Hold you, hold you. (*Breaking* L. *to him.*)

TEGEUS.

We have no chance. It's determined
In section six, paragraph three, of the Regulations.
That has more power than love. It can snuff the great
Candles of creation. It makes me able
To do the impossible, to leave you, to go from the light
That keeps you.

DYNAMENE.

No!

TEGEUS.

O dark, it does. Good-bye,
My memory of earth, my dear most dear
Beyond every expectation. I was wrong
To want you to keep our vows existent
In the vacuum that's coming. It would make you
A heaviness to the world, when you should be,
As you are, a form of light. (*They kiss.* TEGEUS *takes sword
from her, crosses to* R. C.) Dynamene, turn
Your head away. I'm going to let my sword
Solve all the riddles. (*He is about to fall on sword.*)

DYNAMENE.

Chromis, I have it! I know!
Virilius will help you.

TEGEUS.

Virilius?

47

DYNAMENE.

My husband. He can be the other body.

TEGEUS.

Your husband can?

DYNAMENE.

He has no further use
For what he left of himself to lie with us here.
Is there any reason why he shouldn't hang
On your holly tree? Better, far better, he,
Than you who are still alive, and surely better
Than *idling* into corruption?

TEGEUS.

Hang your husband?
Dynamene, it's terrible, horrible.

DYNAMENE.

How little you can understand. I loved
His life not his death. And now we can give his death
The power of life. Not horrible: wonderful!
Isn't it so? That I should be able to feel
He moves again in the world, accomplishing
Our welfare? It's more than my grief could do.

TEGEUS.

What can I say?

DYNAMENE.

That you love me; as I love him
(*Crosses to him.*)
And you. Let's celebrate your safety then.
Where's the bottle? (*Takes bowl which has been at back of
plinth.*) There's some wine unfinished in this bowl.
I'll share it with you. Now forget the fear
We were in; look at me, Chromis. Come away
From the pit you nearly dropped us in. My darling,
I give you Virilius. (*She drinks, passes bowl to* TEGEUS.)

TEGEUS.

Virilius. (*He drinks.*)
And all that follows.

DOTO. (*On the steps, with the bottle.*)
The master. Both the masters.

CURTAIN

48

PROPERTY LIST

Antique oil lamp, of stone or earthenware
Jar with oil for the lamp
A few simple articles of food—bread and perhaps. fruit—and a small
   jar of wine
Soldier's helmet
Soldier's sword
Small bowl
Another similar vessel

SCENE DESIGN
"A PHOENIX TOO FREQUENT"

New

TITLES

ALL OVER TOWN

THE WAGER

SERENADING LOUIE

HARRY OUTSIDE

THE BUTTERFINGERS ANGEL,
MARY & JOSEPH, HEROD THE NUT,
& THE SLAUGHTER OF 12 HIT
CAROLS IN A PEAR TREE

THE KING OF THE UNITED STATES

TADPOLE

THE INTERVIEW

MEL SAYS TO GIVE YOU HIS BEST

A BAD YEAR FOR TOMATOES

THE GIRL WHO LOVED THE BEATLES

THE PIGMAN

● *Write for information*

DRAMATISTS PLAY SERVICE, INC.

440 Park Avenue South   New York, N.Y. 10016

New

 PLAYS

NO MAN'S LAND

LEGEND

FOR THE USE OF THE HALL

THE SORROWS OF FREDERICK

EVERY NIGHT WHEN THE SUN GOES DOWN

DIVORCE—ANYONE?

GRASS WIDOWS

DRACULA

CAVERN OF THE JEWELS (Children's play)

NIGHT THOUGHTS & TERMINAL

GLUTT

UNCLE SNAKE

 DRAMATISTS PLAY SERVICE, INC.
440 Park Avenue South   New York, N.Y. 10016

New
PLAYS

THE PRIMARY ENGLISH CLASS
A GRAVE UNDERTAKING
THE SHORTCHANGED REVIEW
DEMOCRACY
THE TWO-CHARACTER PLAY
SUICIDE—ANYONE?
IT'S SHOWDOWN TIME
NEW BEAT ON AN OLD DRUM
RUBBERS & YANKS 3 DETROIT 0 TOP OF
THE SEVENTH
THE POKEY & THE HORSE LATITUDES
CURTAINS

DRAMATISTS PLAY SERVICE, INC.
440 PARK AVENUE SOUTH   NEW YORK, N.Y. 10016

NEW

Plays

RICH AND FAMOUS

THE RUNNER STUMBLES

THE KRAMER

A FABLE

WHO KILLED RICHARD CORY?

IT'S BEEN WONDERFUL

REGARDING ELECTRA

THE FIRST ACTRESS

SPARED & STAGE DIRECTIONS

THE METAMORPHOSIS

THE AMERICAN WAY (Musical)

DRAMATISTS PLAY SERVICE, INC.
440 PARK AVENUE SOUTH   **NEW YORK, N.Y. 10016**

A PHOENIX
TOO FREQUENT

ACTING EDITION

"To whom conferr'd a peacock's undecent,
A squirrel's harsh, a phoenix too frequent."
Robert Burton quoting Martial.

★

COMEDY IN ONE ACT

BY CHRISTOPHER FRY

★

DRAMATISTS
PLAY SERVICE
INC.